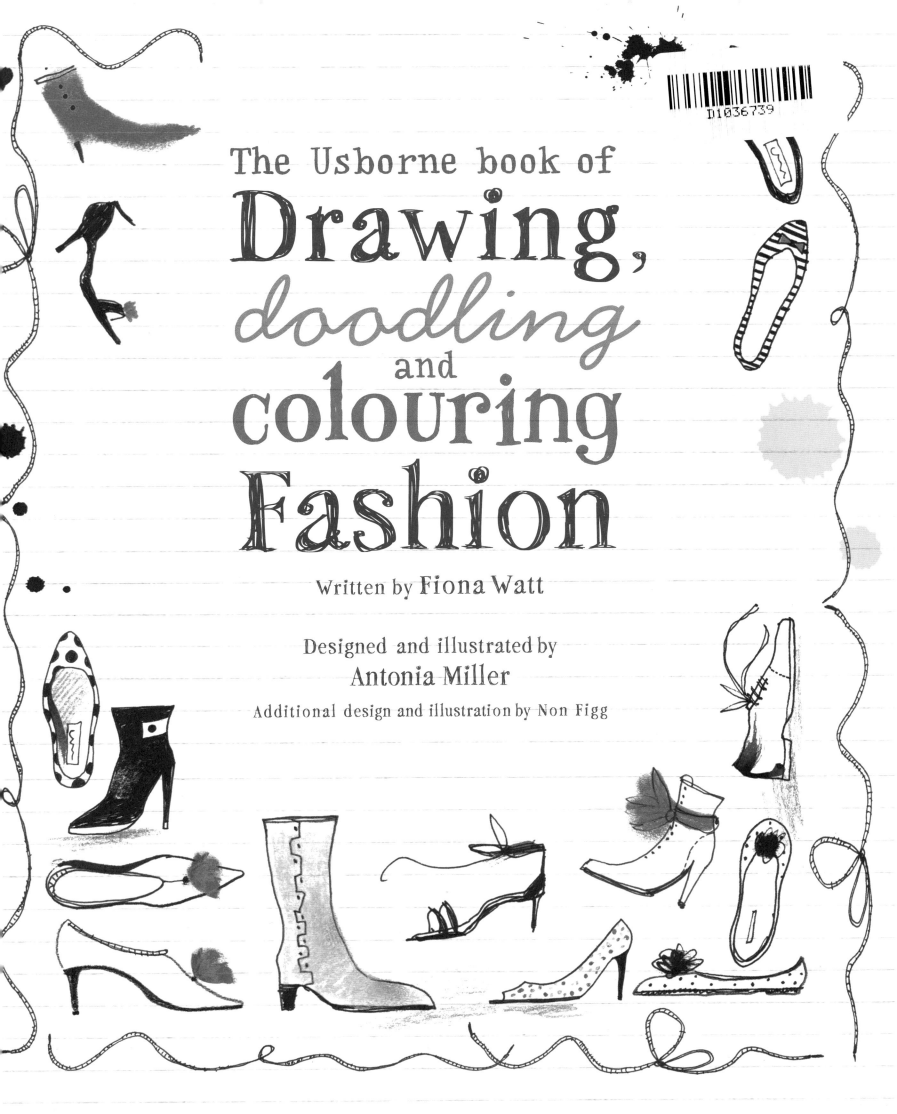

The Usborne book of
Drawing,
doodling
and
colouring
Fashion

Written by **Fiona Watt**

Designed and illustrated by
Antonia Miller

Additional design and illustration by Non Figg

How to use this book...

On some of the pages you'll find ideas for what to do, but you can do whatever you like.

Use pens, pencils or crayons to complete the pictures.

You could fill in large areas, or add patterns of your own.

When you draw on top of a shape with a pen, wait for a couple of seconds for the ink to dry, so that it doesn't smudge.

Some ideas for patterns to doodle...

swirls and curls

circles

spots

geometric

squares

checks

stripes

flowers

Copy these patterns
or create some of
your own...

Striped T-shirts, blue denim,
cool checks – you choose.

Create your own fashion collection by filling in the clothes and accessories.

Designer dolls – what will you dress them in?

A party dress?

A coat and hat?

A T-shirt dress?

A top and skirt?

These girls would like some party make-up.

Designer tip: shade the eye shadow and lipstick with pencils for a soft look.

Party clothes, ballgowns, evening dresses, wedding dresses...

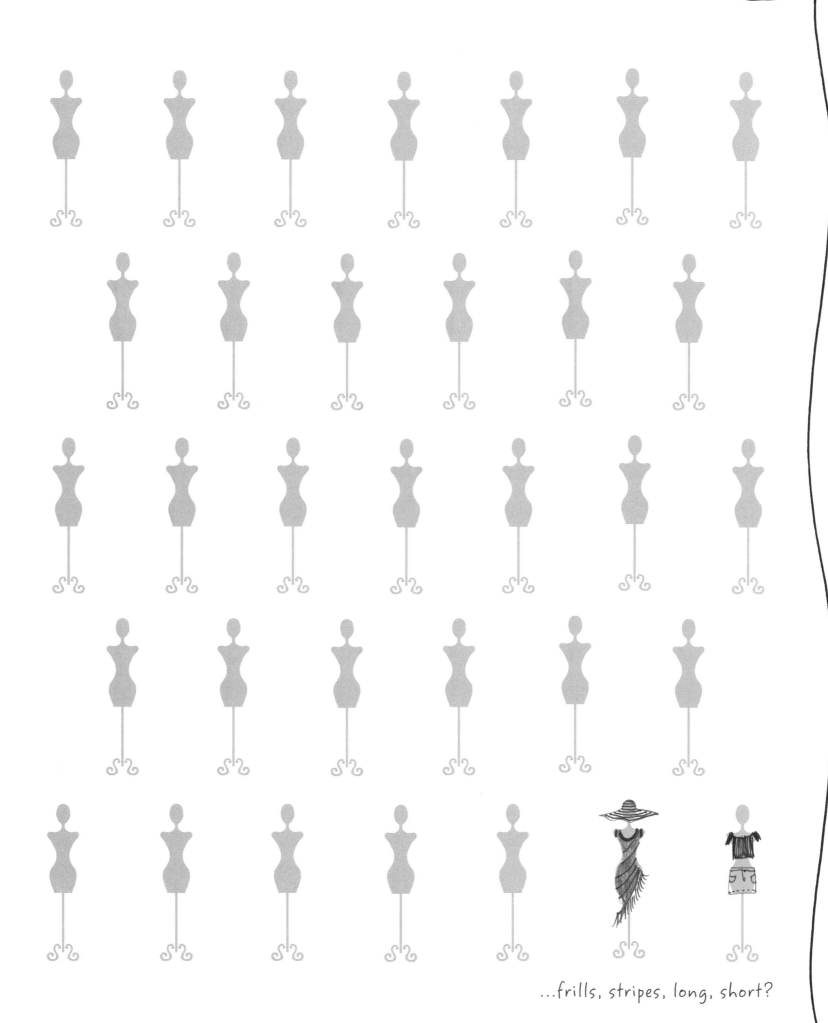

...frills, stripes, long, short?

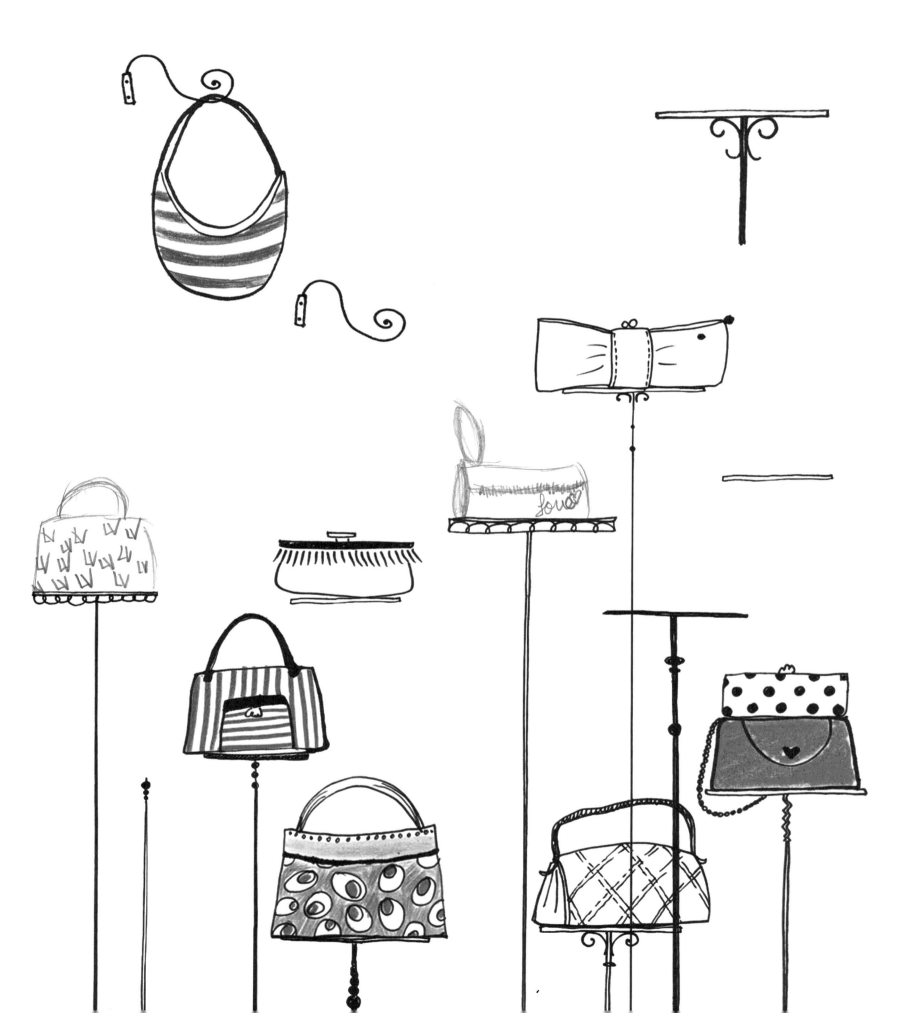

Doodle designer bags on the stands.

Decorate these nails.

Which shades will you choose?

Imagine a double-page feature in a fashion magazine.

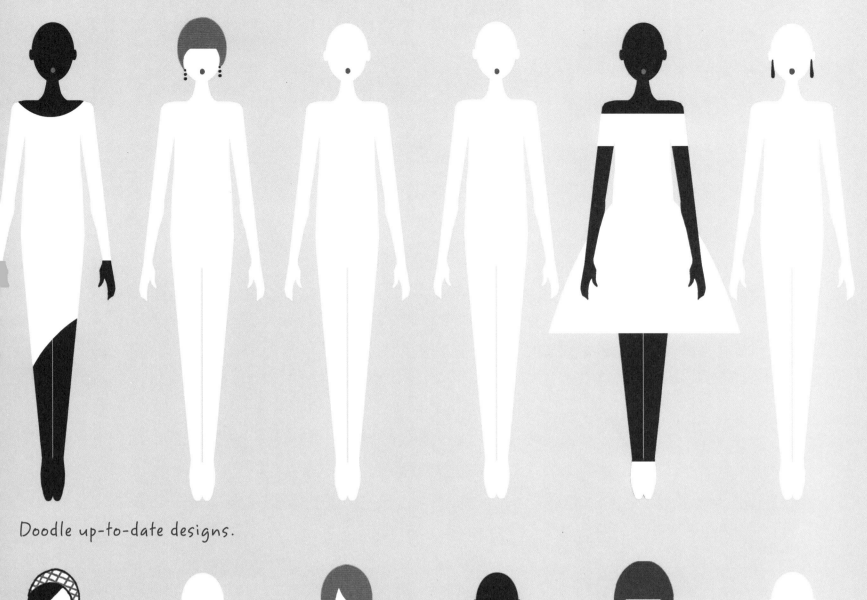

Doodle up-to-date designs.

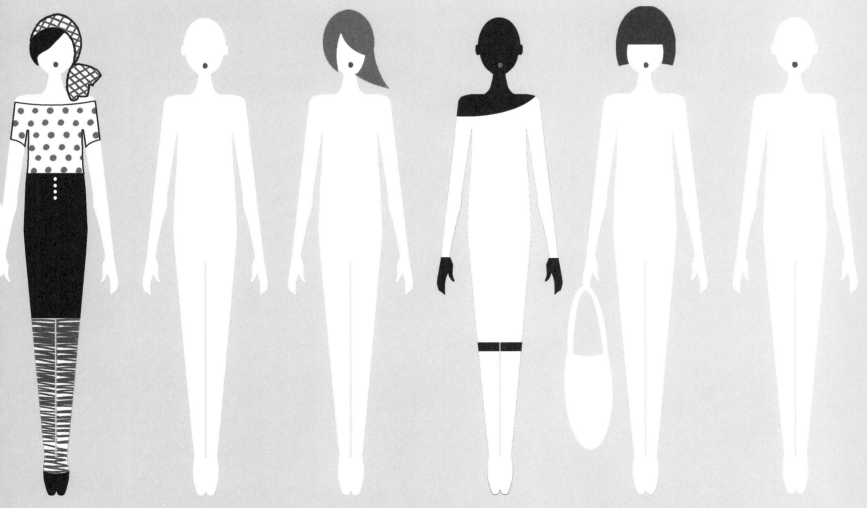

A fabric design for a scarf.

Weekend shopping. Doodle lots of busy shoppers.

Create eye-catching window displays.

What can you buy in each department?

Design some hats for these stylish faces.

A fancy hat with a large brim? A beret? Elegant or a bit crazy?

Use deep or
strong shades for
this winter coat
collection.

Coordinate the
hats and scarves to
match, too.

Draw delicate designs on these elegant dresses from the 1920s.

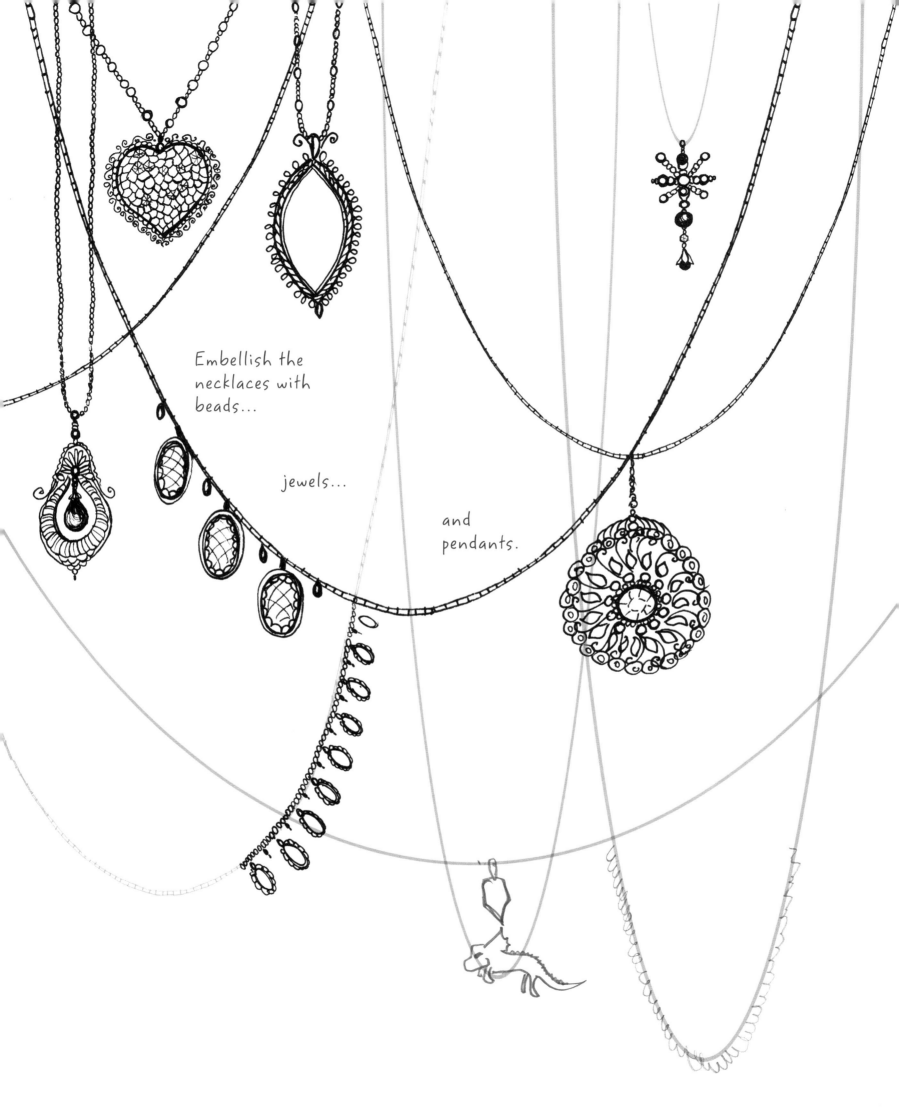

Embellish the necklaces with beads...

jewels...

and pendants.

A girls' night out. What are they wearing?

... and anything else you can think of.

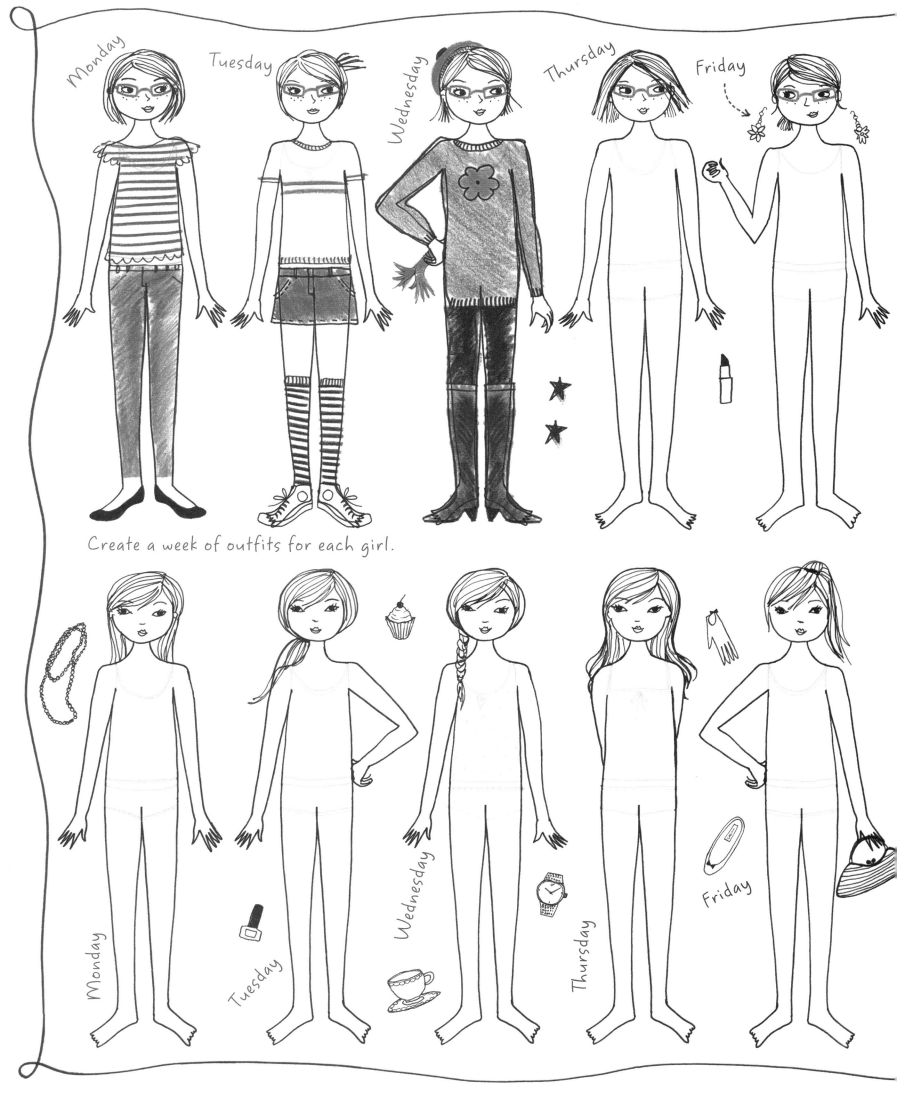

Monday   Tuesday   Wednesday   Thursday   Friday

Create a week of outfits for each girl.

Monday   Tuesday   Wednesday   Thursday   Friday

What will they chose from their wardrobe each day?

Frilly...elegant...flamboyant?
What kind of gloves can you create?

Can you fill the dancing girls' dresses with doodles?

Be a fabric designer
and fill the pages
with patterns.

It's fashion week and the models are under the spotlights... design their outfits.
Are they coordinated or are they all different?

Ankle boots, long boots, flat shoes, high heels, strappy sandals, ballerina pumps...

...fill the pages with them all.

Elegant, sleek, patterned or plain? Doodle outfits on the catwalk models.

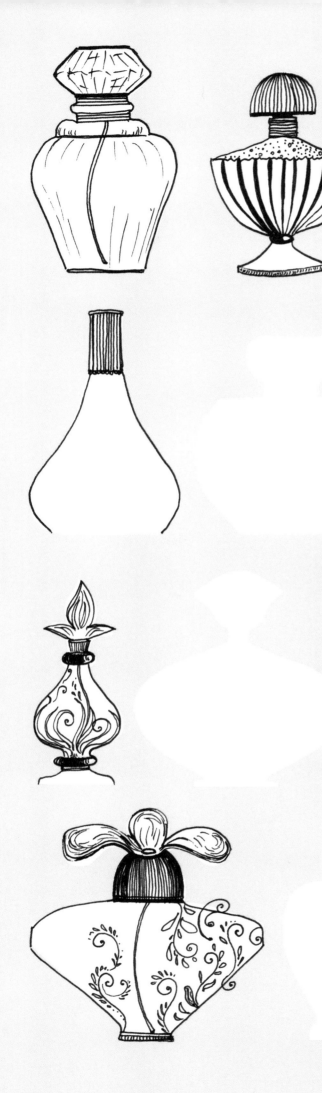

Create a collection of exquisite perfume bottles.

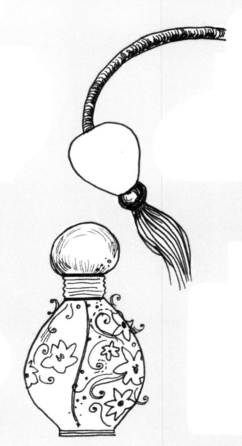

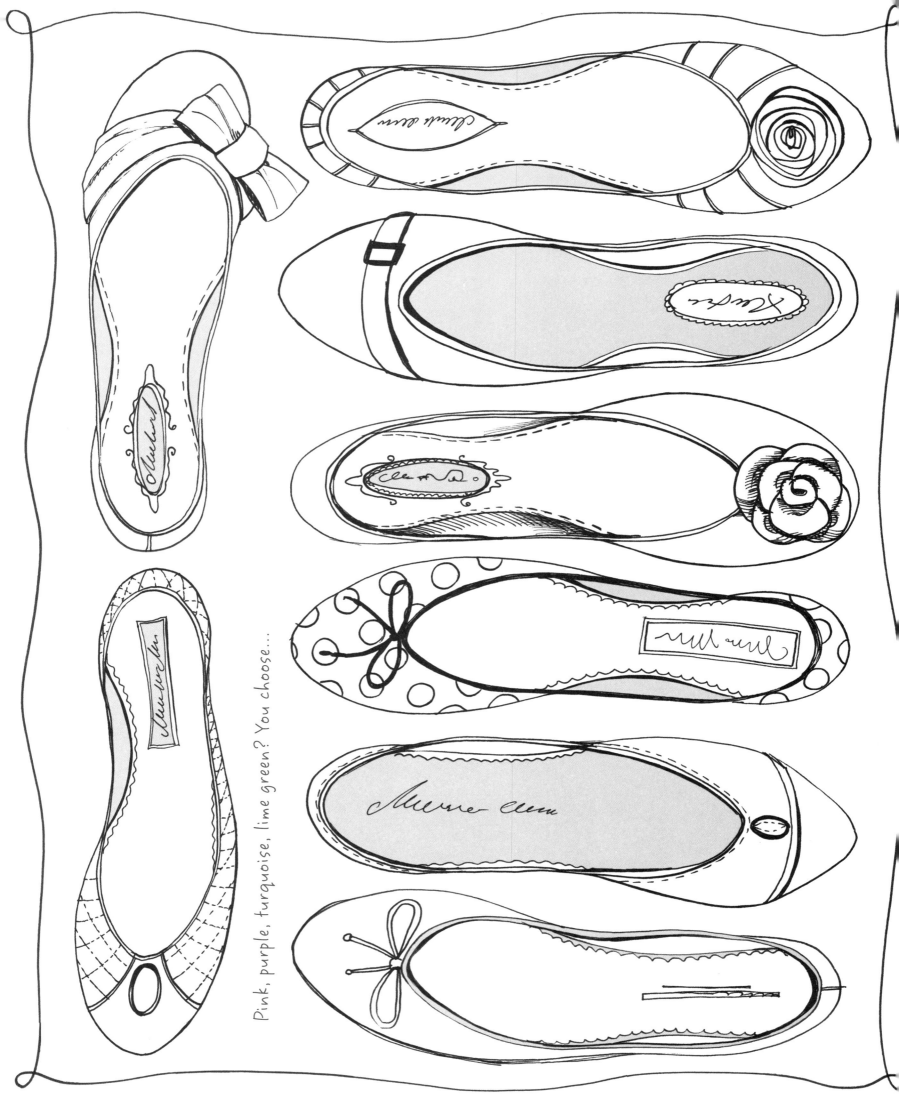

Pink, purple, turquoise, lime green? You choose...

Doodle a different pair of glasses on each face.

Add bows, hair accessories and earrings, too.

Straight...curly...
blond...brunette?
Create different
hairstyles.

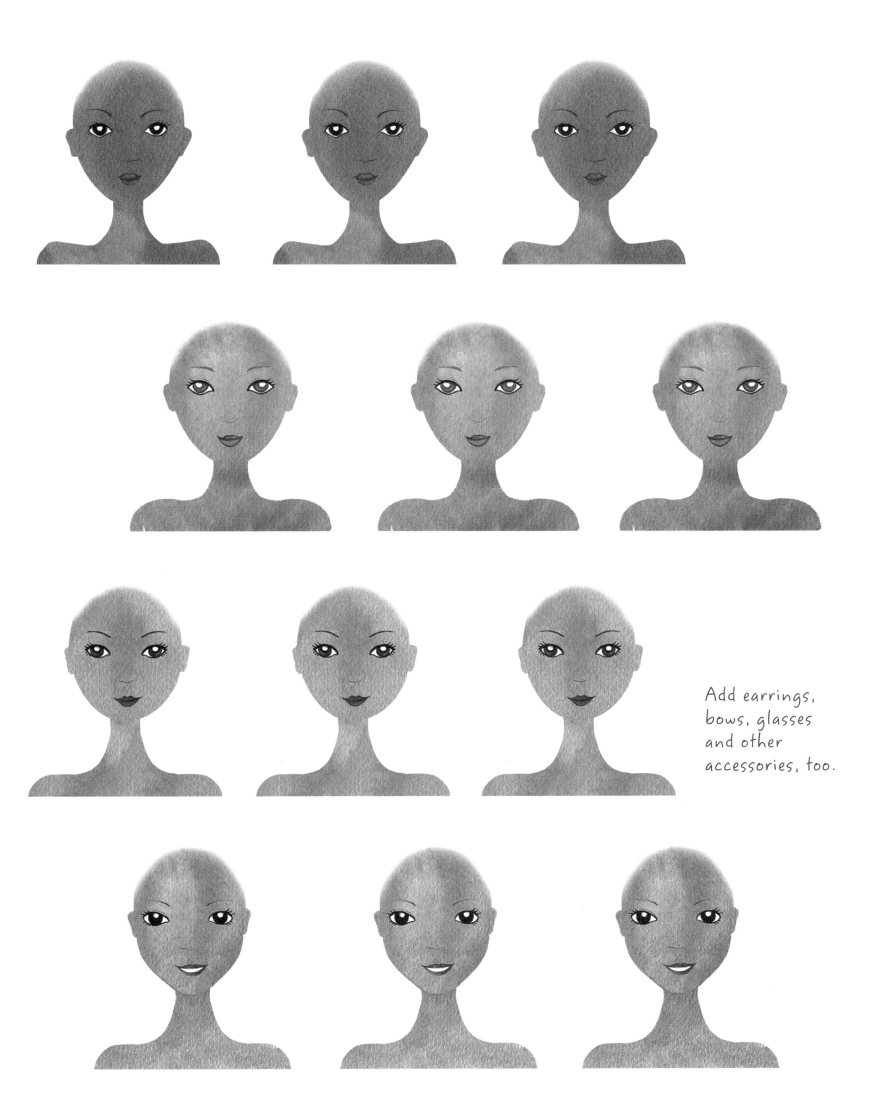

Add earrings,
bows, glasses
and other
accessories, too.

A flowery pattern for a dress fabric.

Guests at a movie premiere. What have they chosen to wear?

Decorate these prom dresses with bows, elegant sashes and dazzling diamanté.

A dressmaker's button box has been knocked over.
Doodle more buttons scattered across the pages.

Lace, silk, satin, taffeta, chiffon or velvet? Sequins, buttons or bows?

Create stylish hats with red and black pens.

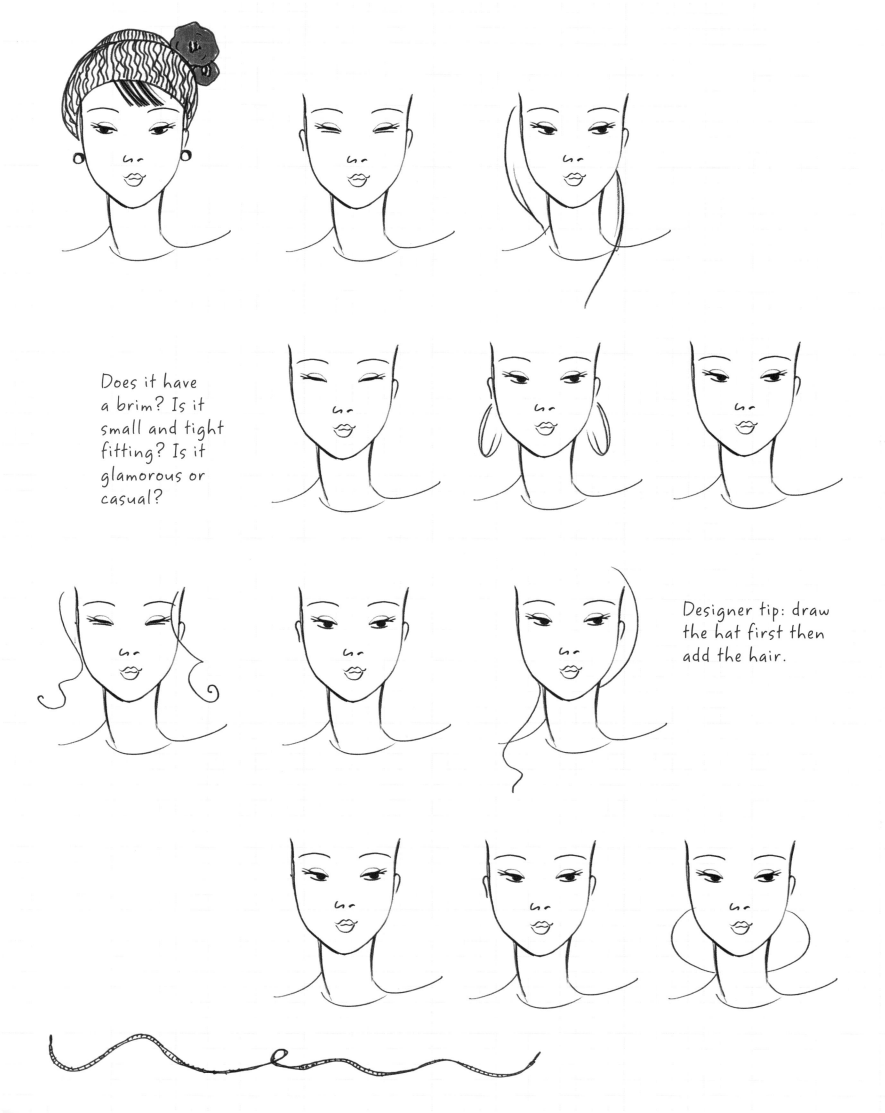

Does it have a brim? Is it small and tight fitting? Is it glamorous or casual?

Designer tip: draw the hat first then add the hair.

Lime green, deep purple, fuschia pink and bright turquoise. Fill in these dresses inspired by fashion in the 1960s.

Fill in the boots, too.

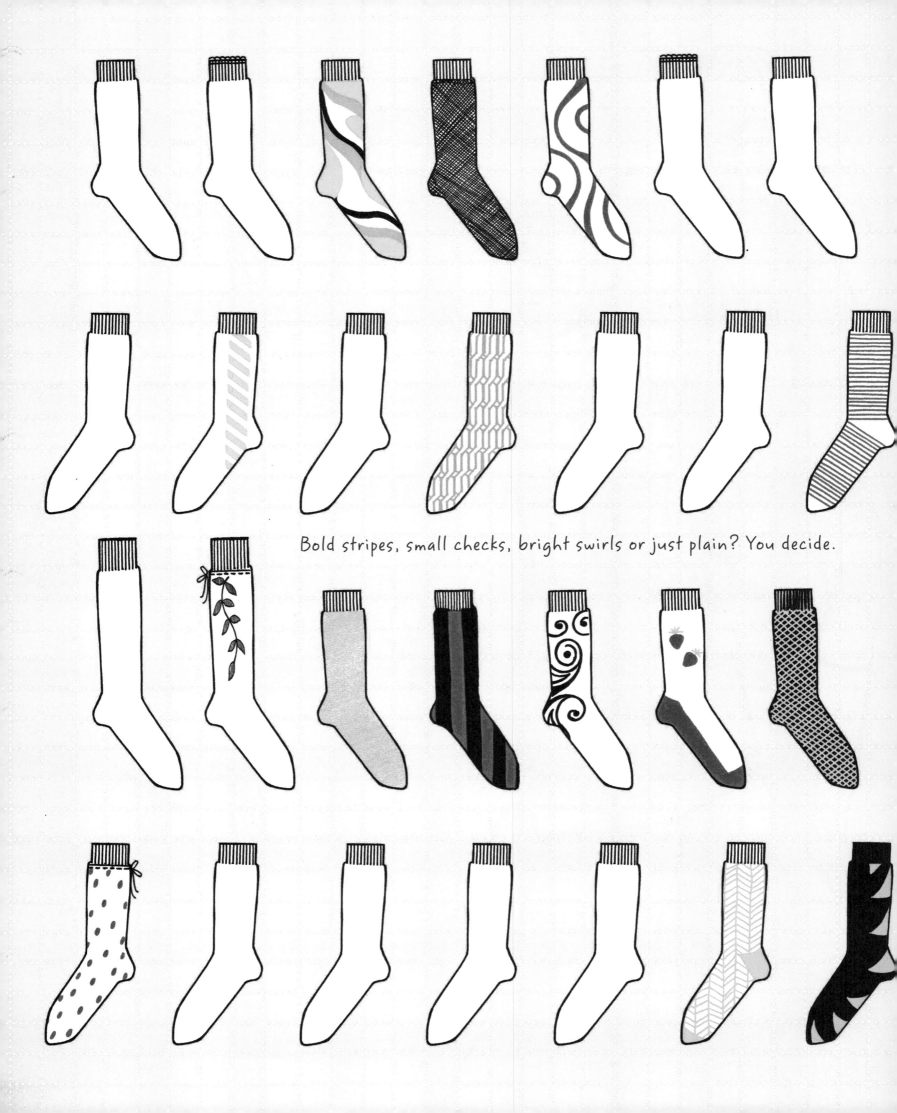

Bold stripes, small checks, bright swirls or just plain? You decide.

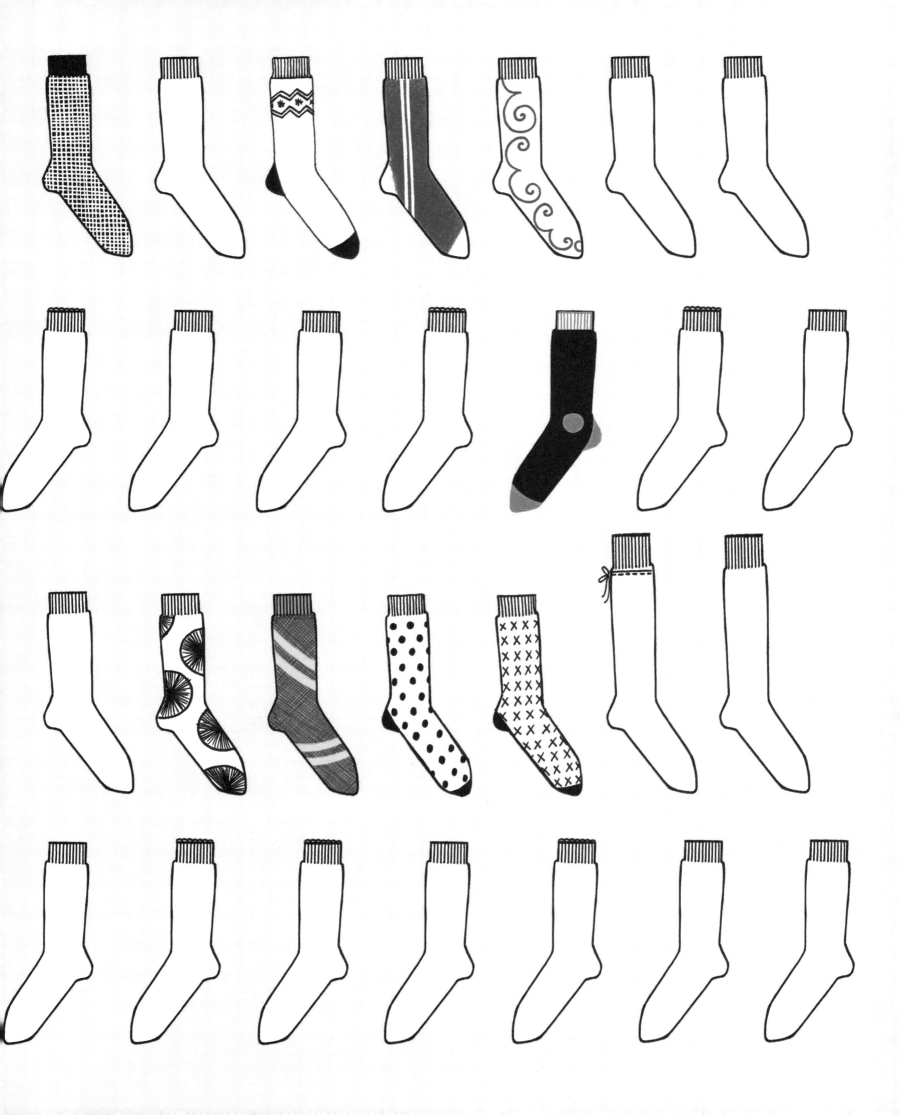

A fashion designer's sketchbook.

Which pattern would you choose for each outfit? Copy the patterns or create new ones.

Design the buildings, then fill the streets with late-night shoppers.

Big, bright, bold patterns, or delicate, pastel designs?
You choose.

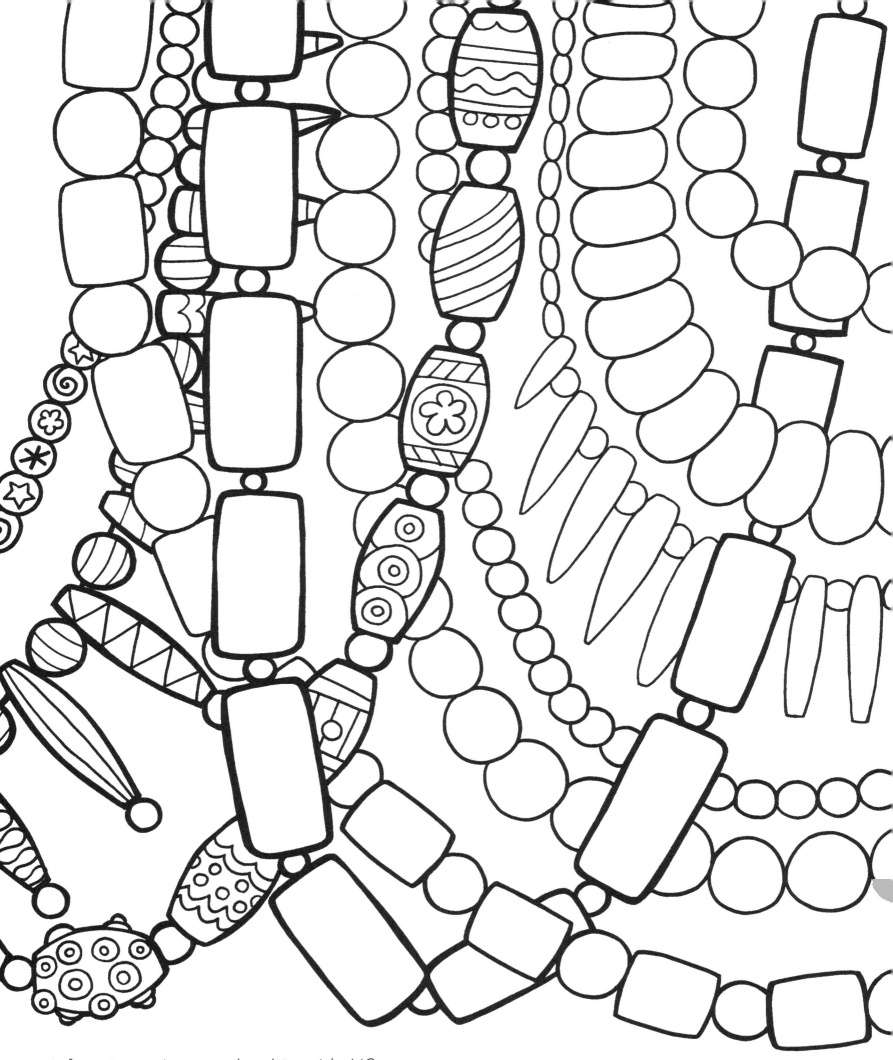

Soft and pastel or very bright and bold?

Choose contrasting shades for this window display.

Doodle patterns on these casual clothes.

You could add some accessories, too.

Doodle designs on these shoes.

Try spots, curls, swirls or anything else you like.

Copy the lacy patterns onto the unfinished squares or design some new ones of your own.

Design a selection of stylish T-shirts for a summer collection.

You could use pinks, purples and soft blues.

Doodle the layers on these stylish flamenco dresses
and add lacy patterns, too.

Faces in the crowd at a catwalk show... doodle more.

Add photographers taking shots of the models.

Create outfits with the
help of the white shapes.

Designer tip: just black and red designs would look smart.

Fill the dressing table with
make-up, hair accessories
and beauty products.